Amazeing
Ancient Treasures

by Joe Tantillo

PANTHEON BOOKS

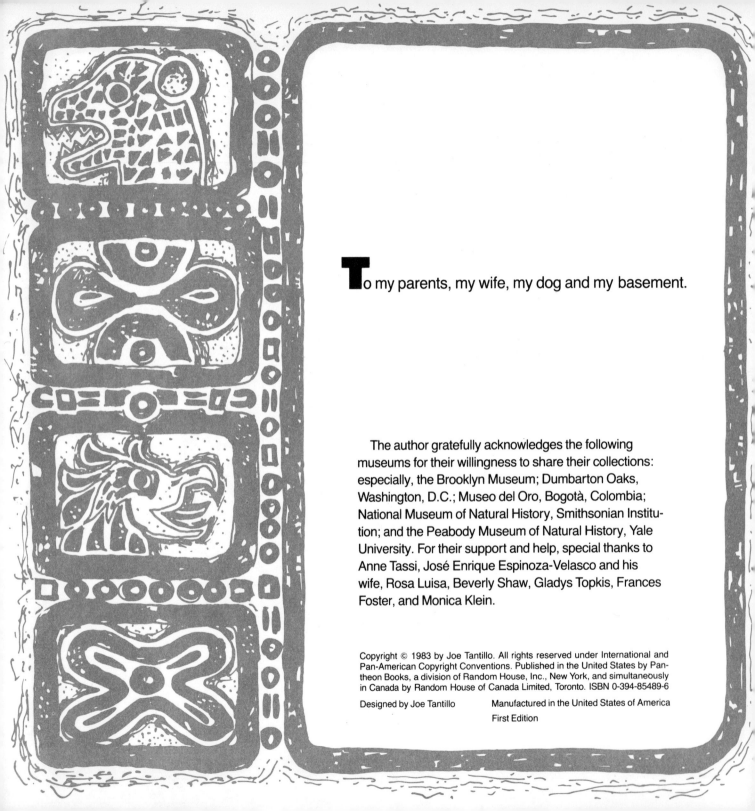

To my parents, my wife, my dog and my basement.

The author gratefully acknowledges the following museums for their willingness to share their collections: especially, the Brooklyn Museum; Dumbarton Oaks, Washington, D.C.; Museo del Oro, Bogotá, Colombia; National Museum of Natural History, Smithsonian Institution; and the Peabody Museum of Natural History, Yale University. For their support and help, special thanks to Anne Tassi, José Enrique Espinoza-Velasco and his wife, Rosa Luisa, Beverly Shaw, Gladys Topkis, Frances Foster, and Monica Klein.

Designed by Joe Tantillo

Manufactured in the United States of America

First Edition

introduction

The mazes in this book are based on artifacts of ancient American civilizations, which were discovered by archaeologists searching the ruins of cities, temples, and tombs in Mexico and South America. The Indians who made these objects were among those Indians from Asia who crossed the land bridge that once existed across the Bering Strait in Alaska and slowly, over many thousands of years, made their way as far south as Chile in South America. The Mexican and South American Indians of the distant past were not unlike the North American Indians; their simple life centered on family and food gathering. Unlike North American Indians, however, some groups developed great civilizations, as great as those of Egypt, Rome, and Greece—among them, the Aztecs, the Mayans, and the Incas. These groups arose from other lesser known tribes—the Toltecs, the Zapotecs, the Mixtecs, the Olmecs, and many others.

Many of these tribes were extinct by the time Columbus sailed to the new land that he thought of as the "New World"—actually, it was an "Old World" indeed. The classic Mayan civilization lasted from A.D. 300 until a little past A.D. 900. Older cultures such as the Wairajuca were long gone by 1800 B.C. But we can learn about these people from the objects they left behind. What did they use to carry water? What did they make, and why? These are the artifacts presented in this book. Some were practical, like the Peruvian pottery jars, and others were part of tribal worship, statues of their gods. Some were made of stone and others of jade and gold.

It was rumors of this gold that first interested the *conquistadors,* the Spanish adventurers who explored the regions of Mexico, Central America, and northwestern South America in the sixteenth century. The greed for gold led to the quick destruction of the mighty empires of the Aztecs and Incas by a few ruthless men. The conquest ended many native traditions and customs as the tribes were crushed under Spanish rule.

As you work your way through the mazes, take a moment to think about the craftspeople of old who pounded, shaped, and carved these pieces.

Happy mazing.

maze
one

Begin at the ☐ and
work through to the ◪

**Solution to maze one found
on the following page.**

Mixtec gold deity

maze
two

Begin at the O and
work through to the ●

Solution to maze one

**Incan silver
llama figurines**

maze
three

Begin at the ▽ and
work through to the ▼

Solution to maze two

Peruvian clay jar

maze
four

Begin at the ⟁ and
work through to the ●●

Solution to maze three

Mixtec gold pendant

maze
five

Begin at the ⇨ and
work through to the ➡

Solution to maze four

Mayan urn

maze
six

Begin at the ✛ and
work through to the ◎

Solution to maze five

**Colombian carved clay
musical instrument**

maze
seven

Begin at the ✠ and
work through to the ✠

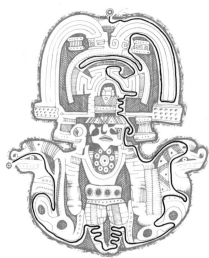

Solution to maze six

Mexican slate mirror

© Joe Tantillo 1983

maze
eight

Begin at the □ and
work through to the ▧

Solution to maze seven

Mayan stone carving

maze
nine

Begin at the **X** and
work through to the **O**

Solution to maze eight

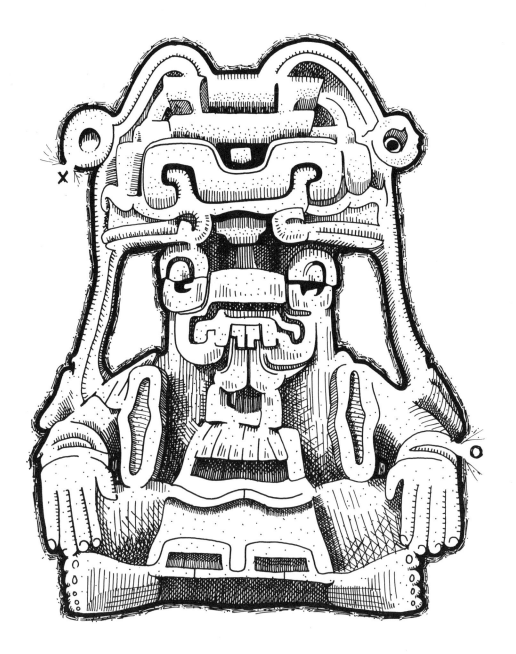

Zapotec rain god, Cocijo

© Joe Tantillo 1983

maze
ten

Find the path from one
O to the center ●

Solution to maze nine

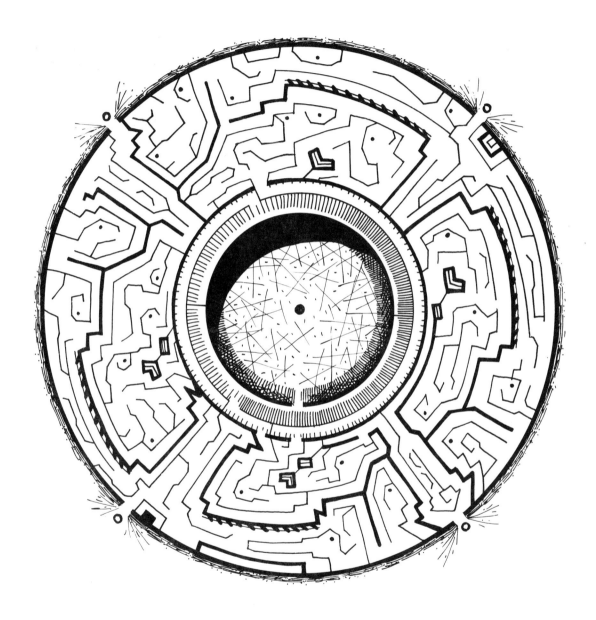

Peruvian clay pot

maze
eleven

Begin at the bottom ⌂ and
work through to the top ⌂

Solution to maze ten

Peruvian clay mask

maze twelve

Begin at the ⩔ and
work through to the ⩔

**Solution to maze
eleven**

**Peruvian hammered
gold plaque**

maze
thirteen

Begin at the ✚ and
work through to the ✦

Solution to maze
twelve

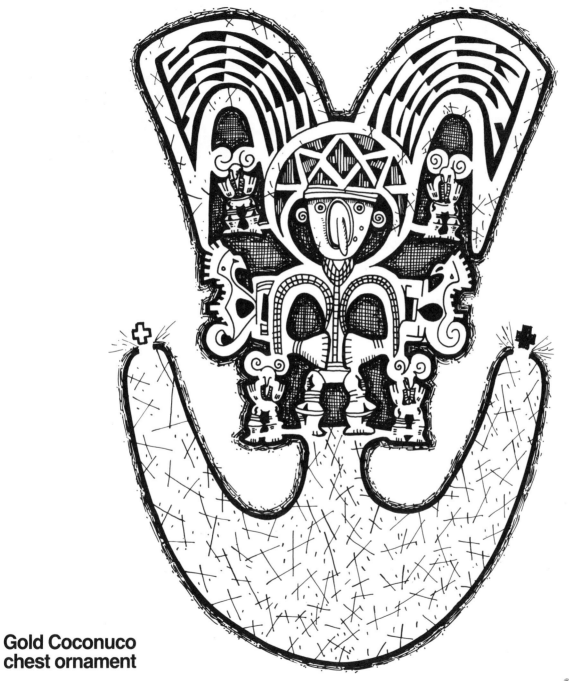

**Gold Coconuco
chest ornament**

© Joe Tantillo 1983

maze
fourteen

Find the path from either
△ to the ▲

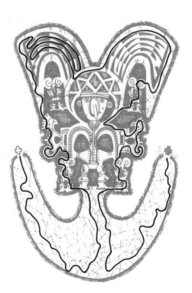

Solution to maze
thirteen

**Colombian gold
chest ornament**

maze
fifteen

Begin at the ✘ and
work through to the ✘

**Solution to maze
fourteen**

Chavin gold jaguar

maze
sixteen

Begin at the 〉〉 left and
work through to the 〉〉 right

**Solution to maze
fifteen**

Monte Alban clay urn

© Joe Tantillo 1983

maze
seventeen

Begin at the and
work through to the

**Solution to maze
sixteen**

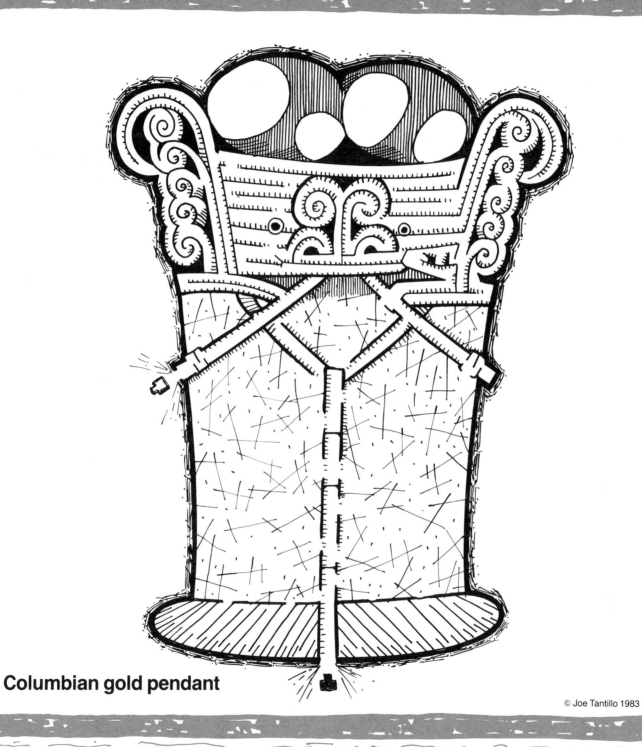

Columbian gold pendant

© Joe Tantillo 1983

maze eighteen

Begin at the □ and
work through to the ▮

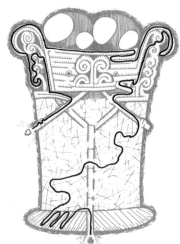

**Solution to maze
seventeen**

Huaxtec stone statue

© Joe Tantillo 1983

maze
nineteen

Begin at the ▶▶ left and
work through to the ▶▶ bottom

**Solution to maze
eighteen**

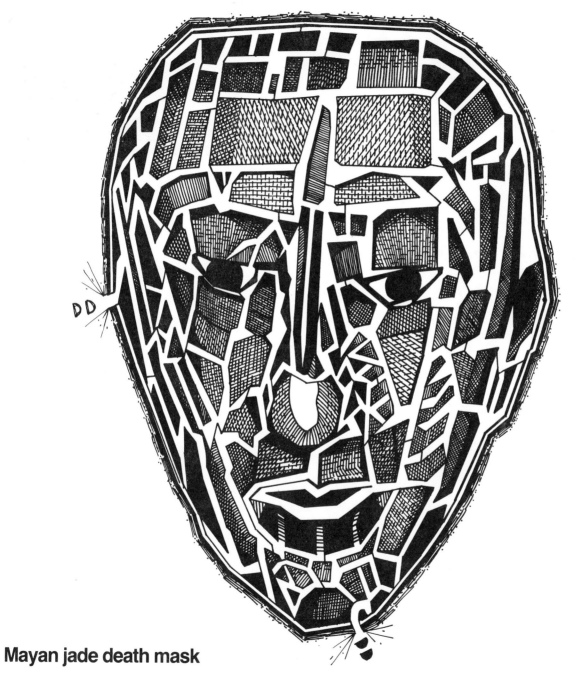

DD

Mayan jade death mask

© Joe Tantillo 1983

maze
twenty

Begin at the ✛ and
work through to the ✛✛

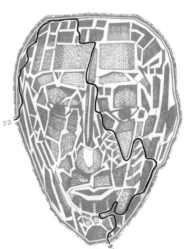

**Solution to maze
nineteen**

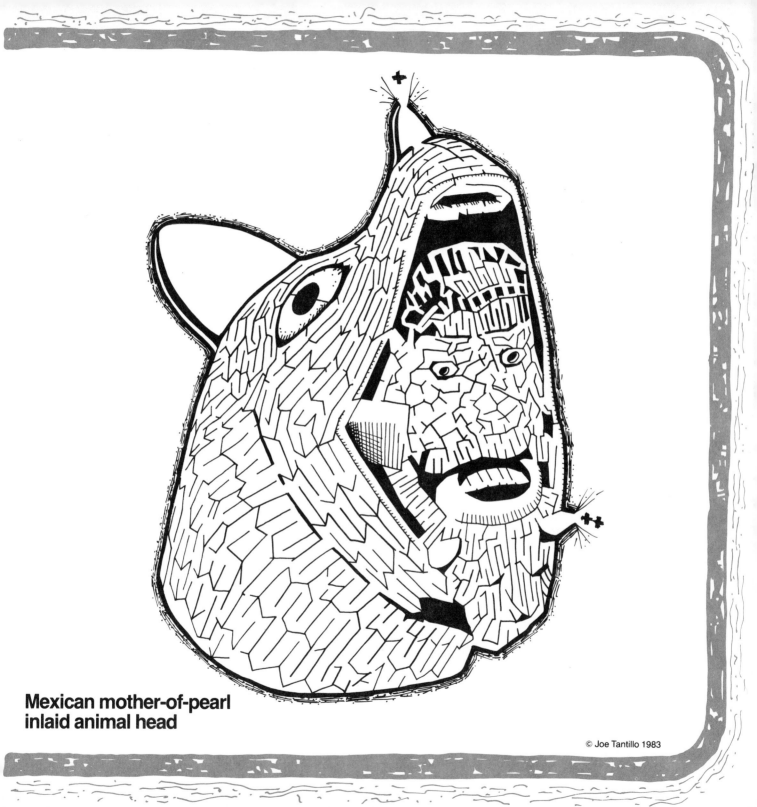

**Mexican mother-of-pearl
inlaid animal head**

© Joe Tantillo 1983

maze twenty-one

Begin at the ✤ left and work through to the ✤ right

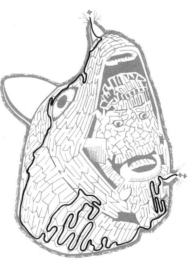

Solution to maze twenty

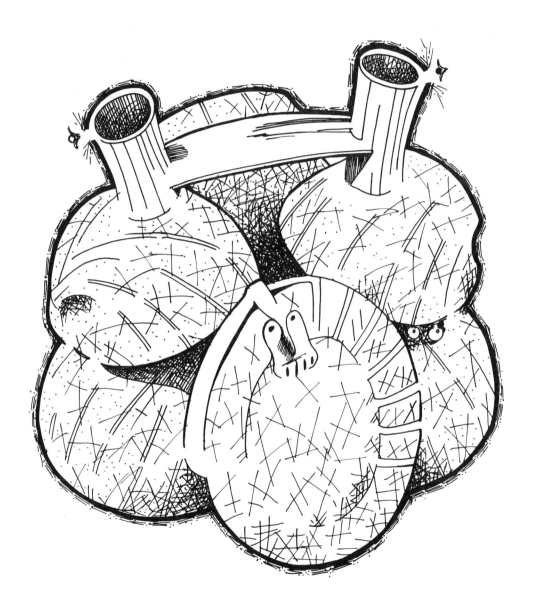

Peruvian clay jar

maze twenty- two

Begin at the □ and
work through to the ▣

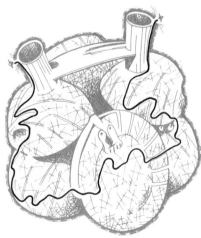

**Solution to maze
twenty-one**

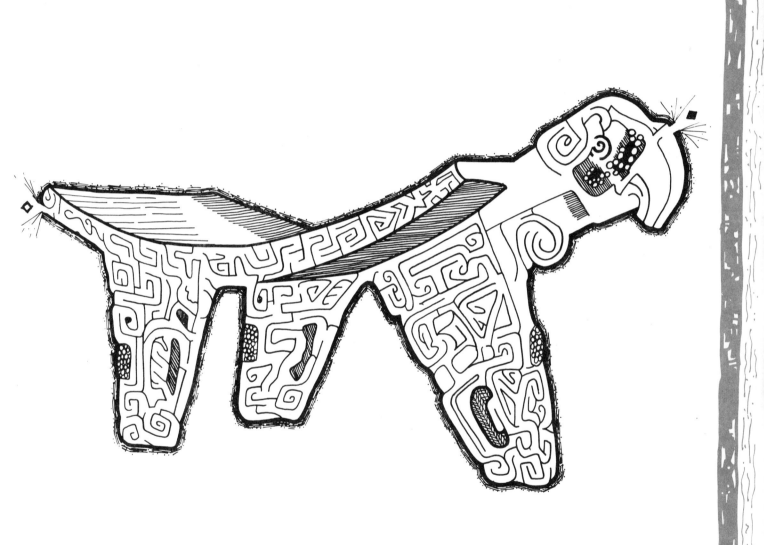

**Costa Rican volcanic
stone carving**

© Joe Tantillo 1983

maze twenty- three

Begin at the ◆ and work through to the ◈

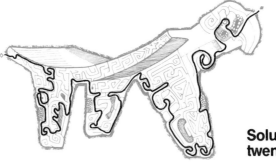

Solution to maze twenty-two

**Costa Rican
gold ornament**

© Joe Tantillo 1983

maze
twenty-four

Find the path from either
☆ to the ☆

**Solution to maze
twenty-three**

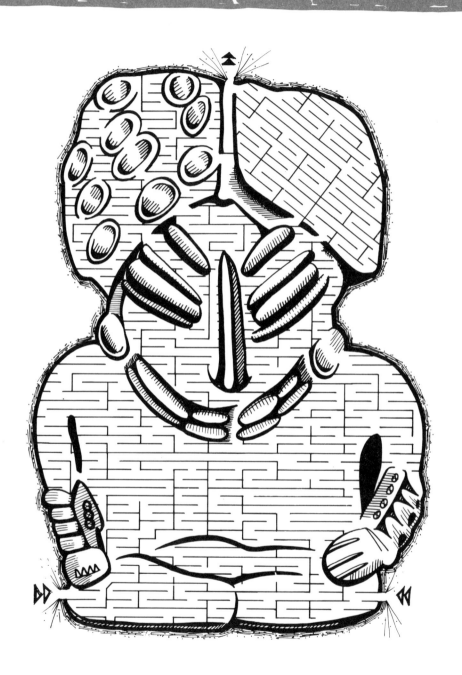

**Chupicuaro
clay figure**

maze
twenty-
five

Begin at the X and
work through to the XX

**Solution to maze
twenty-four**

**Mexican turquoise and
shell mosaic**

© Joe Tantillo 1983

maze twenty-six

Begin at the X and
work through to the XX

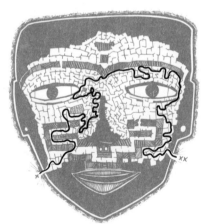

**Solution to maze
twenty-five**

Mayan stone carving

maze twenty-seven

Begin at the O
work through to the ♦

Solution to maze twenty-six

Mexican ceremonial brazier

maze twenty-eight

Begin at the ◇ and work through to the ◆

Solution to maze twenty-seven

Jalisco clay figures

maze twenty-nine

Begin at the ✕ and
work through to the ✕✕

**Solution to maze
twenty-eight**

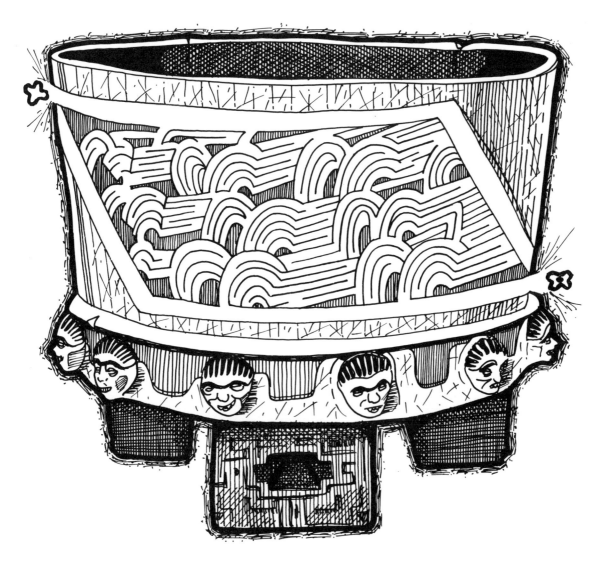

Mexican three-footed clay pot

maze thirty

Begin at the >> left and
work through to the >> right

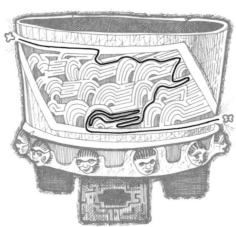

**Solution to maze
twenty-nine**

Mexican pottery head

Solution to maze thirty.

about the author

Joe Tantillo is a graphic designer and illustrator who owns a graphic design studio in Hamden, Connecticut. In 1974 he graduated from the Syracuse University School of Visual and Performing Arts with a B.F.A. in illustration. *Amazeing Ancient Treasures* is the merging of his love of art history and his longtime interest in mazes. In addition to creating mazes, he builds and flies radio-controlled airplanes and makes musical instruments. His paintings have been widely exhibited. He lives with his wife Maura, and his dog Kristi, in North Haven, Connecticut.